Amazing butterfly

How long do butterflies live for a lepidopterist? Find the answers below.

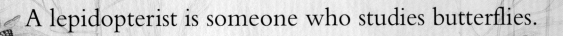

Male butterflies are often more colourful than female ones.

Butterflies cannot fly if their body temperature is too cold. That is why they are mostly seen on sunny days.

A lepidopterist is someone who studies butterflies.

Moths are usually less colourful than butterflies, have hairier bodies, keep their wings out when resting and mostly fly at night.

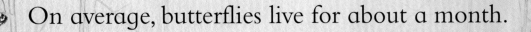

On average, butterflies live for about a month.

Butterflies are called "schmetterling" in German, "papillon" in French and "sommerfug" in Danish.

Antarctica is the only place where there are no butterflies.

Butterfly-spotters, turn the page!

small white

Easy-to-spot butterflies

Do you recognise any of these butterflies?
These are the ones you are most likely to see.

gatekeeper ○

small white ○

holly blue ○

○ comma

speckled wood ○

green-veined white ○

small tortoiseshell ○

large white ○

wall ○

LET'S LOOK FOR BUTTERFLIES

HOW TO USE THIS BOOK

On a sunny day, there is no better way to while away the time than to look for butterflies. The best time to see them is in the spring and summer when this guide can help you to ...

... find out all about these incredible insects and the things that make them so amazing.

adonis blue

... identify different types of butterflies (it can be quite tricky), then tick off the ones you see.

... have fun colouring the butterflies and playing with the stickers on the fold-out meadow scene at the back.

Looking at butterflies

Butterflies are insects. This means they have six legs and their bodies are made up of three sections – the head, thorax and abdomen.

PARTS OF A BUTTERFLY

Feelers
These help the butterfly taste its food. Look for the thicker bit at the end.

Head

Eyes

Thorax
This middle bit of the body can be thick or thin, hairy or smooth.

Abdomen
A butterfly is covered in tiny scales right down to its abdomen. This is the end section of its body.

Wings
Butterflies are often colourful to attract mates, but some are dull to help them hide.

Tick the butterflies off as you find them.

Harder-to-spot butterflies

Essex skipper ◯

green hairstreak ◯

chalkhill blue ◯

marbled white ◯

clouded yellow ◯

brown argus ◯

small skipper ◯

dingy skipper ◯

adonis blue

dark green
fritillary

white
admiral

small blue

silver-washed
fritillary

heath fritillary

purple hairstreak

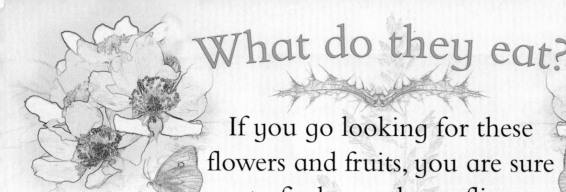

What do they eat?

If you go looking for these flowers and fruits, you are sure to find some butterflies.

Wild flowers
Search for butterflies on the flowers that grow in the fields, woods and hedgerows.

Knapweed and nettles
Both these plants attract butterflies, especially on a warm day.

Garden plants
Gardens are great places to find butterflies. They love this plant called buddleia.

Bramble flowers and berries
Butterflies, like this comma, feed on bramble flowers in summer and blackberries in autumn.

Rotting fruit
Unlike us, some butterflies happily feed on rotting fruit, like this red admiral.

The egg and the butterfly

How does a tiny egg turn into a beautiful butterfly? This is one of the strangest animal stories.

2. Tiny caterpillars hatch out of the eggs.

1. A butterfly lays some eggs on a leaf.

3. The hungry caterpillars eat and eat and eat.

6. Finally, it breaks free, dries its wings and flies away.

5. ...it forms a hard case. Inside the case, it slowly turns into a butterfly.

4. Each caterpillar gets bigger and bigger until...